BREAKTHROUGH

FROM A GIFTED COMPUTER TO BUILDING A MOVEMENT THAT SAVES LIVES

MOHAMED AZVAN SAIT

To my beloved parents, whose steadfast support and encouragement have been the bedrock for every courageous step I've dared to take. Your belief in me has fueled my journey and inspired me to chase my dreams with fervor.

To every young dreamer out there, those of you who are feeling uncertain, exploring new possibilities, or navigating through feelings of confusion, I dedicate this book to you. May these pages ignite a spark within you, guiding you toward your own moments of clarity and breakthrough. Embrace your journey, for it is uniquely yours, and let it lead you to the extraordinary.

Contents

Foreword

In the world of startups, entrepreneurship is a journey of continuous transformation - one that demands resilience, vision, and the courage to confront the unknown. Azvan Sait's story is a powerful reminder of what it takes to not only dream big but to follow through with unwavering commitment. As I reflect on his remarkable journey, it's an honor to write the foreword to his book, which captures the essence of his entrepreneurial evolution, from a simple idea to a life-changing reality.

Our connection began at a Hackathon named Web It Up, organized by Steyp in association with Grolius at Carmel Engineering College, Alappuzha. I had the privilege of addressing the students on career development, skill-building, and the power of pursuing meaningful, impactful ideas, particularly in the startup space. Azvan was among the audience that day, and my words sparked something within him - an ambition to step into the world of startups and make a difference. It was a moment of inspiration that set the stage for what was to come.

Some months later, Azvan reached out to me, sharing his vision for a startup aimed at bridging the gap between blood donors and recipients. His concept was rooted in a simple yet profound mission: to make blood donation more accessible, efficient, and life-saving. What stood out was Azvan's deep passion for the cause, and I knew that with the right guidance, he could shape this idea into something truly impactful.

As his mentor, my role was to push Azvan to refine his vision, challenge assumptions, and explore new possibilities. We worked tirelessly to turn his idea into a solid startup model. Through countless discussions and brainstorming sessions, both in person and online, we navigated the complexities of building a startup - identifying strengths, addressing weaknesses, and ensuring that his concept was ready for the market.

When it came time to present Purelink to the co-founder at Talrop, I knew that Azvan's startup was more than just an idea - it was a vision that could make a real difference. Today, Purelink is part of the Talrop startup ecosystem, helping to reshape the way blood donation is managed. This is not just a success story; it is a testament to the power of mentorship, perseverance, and the willingness to take bold steps towards a bigger purpose.

Azvan's journey, as chronicled in this book, is an inspiring one. It is a story of growth, challenges, and triumphs. His experiences will inspire anyone with an idea to take action, believe in their vision, and never give up on their dreams, no matter how daunting the path may seem. This is more than just a startup story - it is a story of personal evolution and the incredible impact that entrepreneurship can have on both individuals and society.

-Adhil Muhammad
Founder & CEO, Aidmak

Preface

We often underestimate the moments that change our lives. For me, it wasn't a grand event — it was a quiet evening during the pandemic, sitting in front of a computer that had more potential than I realized. A simple question sparked it all: "What more can I do with this?"

That question led me down a path I never imagined: from exploring ethical hacking to designing a blood donation platform, from watching YouTube tutorials to pitching ideas to real CEOs, from being just another student to becoming a startup founder.

This book isn't just about a startup. It's about discovering your own potential in unexpected places. It's about the courage to try something new even when you're young, inexperienced, or unsure.

To every young person reading this: the age you are now is not a limitation; it's your greatest opportunity.

Use it well.

Acknowledgements

No journey worth telling is ever walked alone. Behind every chapter in this book are individuals who believed in me before I believed in myself.

To my parents, your faith and encouragement were my launchpad. You listened to every idea, every frustration, and every wild plan without ever dimming my fire.

To Sobir sir, CEO of Steyp, thank you for creating an ecosystem where young minds could grow. Your guidance helped shape my confidence in tech.

To Safeer sir, CEO of Talrop, your insights transformed the future of PureLink. Your words showed me what scale truly means.

To Adhil Muhammad and the Grolius team, that hackathon changed everything. Thank you for inspiring me with your journey and helping me take my first step.

To my incredible co-founders and the team behind PureLink, none of this would be real without you.

To every friend, mentor, and well-wisher who offered a word of support, a moment of clarity, or a much-needed reality check, thank you.

This book is as much yours as it is mine.

Prologue

They say the teenage years are confusing. They were for me, too. But confusion isn't the end, it's the beginning of curiosity. And curiosity, when given a direction, can spark revolutions.

In 2022, I moved back to Kerala, my birthplace. I had no roadmap, just a deep interest in cybersecurity and technology. That interest led me to Steyp, an initiative I discovered through a YouTube video by Farhan Bin Fazil. Steyp's tech schooling course was where things truly began.

Then came the hackathon in Alappuzha, organized by Steyp and Grolius. It was there, while researching blood donation awareness, that I saw a gap, a real problem that needed solving. The idea for PureLink was born, not from a desire to build a company, but from a desire to solve something meaningful.

From that point on, the story changed. There were late-night calls, prototype failures, self-doubt, excitement, meetings with mentors, and brainstorming with co-founders. And through it all, one thing stayed constant, the desire to keep going.

"The moment you stop learning, you stop growing. Stay curious, stay hungry."

It's the story of someone who started. Who learned. Who grew. And who is still moving forward. This is my breakthrough.

CHAPTER ONE

ROOTS OF A DREAM

I'm Mohamed Azvan Sait, and this is the story of how a young boy with no clue about tech, startups, or hacking found his path in the heart of Kerala, one line of code at a time. I was born in Kochi, Kerala, India and moved to Saudi Arabia at the age of 4. We're a middle-class family with strong bonds and big dreams. I have two siblings and my parents who have always believed in me, even when I didn't fully believe in myself.

I was never the top student in class. In fact, I was quite the opposite, mediocre. But I was always curious. I participated in everything sports, arts, debates. Just to find where I belonged. I wasn't good at sports, but I learned one important thing from trying them: I had a hardworking, dedicated soul. Even though I wasn't great at arts, I still found joy in it. My interest wasn't in video games either, unlike most kids my age. Back then, I had no deep awareness about the world of technology. Life was simple, surrounded by good friends, happy moments, and a lot of exploration.

"Curiosity may not make you the best at everything, but it makes you unstoppable at becoming better than yesterday."

Everything changed when I received my first computer. It was a gift from my father's friend. He noticed that spark in me, the curiosity. At first, I did what most kids would do: watched entertainment videos. Then came the COVID-19 pandemic, and like many, I was locked inside with a lot of time and a curious mind.

One day, I stumbled upon a trick where you could make the Command Prompt look like a hacker's tool. I showed it to my siblings, all proud. But that moment lit a fire inside me. I asked myself, "How do you really hack?" And that question took me down a rabbit hole.

I discovered ethical hacking. That it was not only legal but could also be a career. I switched from watching random videos to consuming content from creators like Null Byte and NetworkChuck. That's when I realized: IT is my thing. This is where I belong.

CHAPTER TWO

THE CUBE AND THE CODE WITHIN

During the long stillness of the COVID-19 lockdown, something unexpected sparked a fire inside me.

One day, a classmate shared a video in our group, showing himself solving a Rubik's Cube in under a minute. I was stunned. It wasn't just a flashy trick, it felt like he had unlocked a hidden code. Eager and inspired, I messaged him, hoping to learn how he did it.

But he refused to share his method.

I felt disappointed. I wasn't asking for praise, I just wanted to learn. It felt like a door was slammed shut right when I had reached for the handle. I remember staring at my own Rubik's Cube, confused, frustrated, and unsure.

That's when my father, seeing my disappointment, said something that changed everything:

"Azvan is the only one capable of doing what Azvan can do. So if he doesn't tell you his method, find your own."

That line wasn't just a comfort, it was a spark. It ignited something within me. His words made me believe that I could do it on my own.

So, I did.

I started watching YouTube tutorials, piecing together different solving methods, trying and failing again and again. Days passed, and then... it clicked. The cube twisted into place, every color aligned. I had done it. And within a few more days, I was solving it in under a minute, just like the video that had once discouraged me.

But this time, it wasn't about proving something to anyone.
It was about discovering what I was capable of when I chose not to stop.

That one incident taught me a lifelong lesson: *you don't need someone else's path to succeed, you can carve your own.*

CHAPTER THREE

Finding My Tribe: The Steyp Era

Some of the most beautiful turns in life begin not with a major decision, but with a random scroll, a click, a spark. For me, it was a video by Farhan Bin Fazil that did the magic. I wasn't even looking for anything serious that day. Just another evening, scrolling through Instagram. But the moment he started talking about Steyp, a tech learning platform, something about his words stuck with me.

He spoke about how Steyp was redefining the way young people learn technology. Not just with theory, but by building real things. That was all I needed to hear.

That night, I couldn't sleep properly. I kept thinking about it "What if this is for me?" The next morning, I found myself deep into Steyp's website. I explored everything, courses, mentors, student reviews. One course stood out like a shining light: Full-stack Development.

It felt like a doorway into the world I'd been dreaming of, the world where you don't just use technology, you build it.

Around the same time, we shifted back to Kochi, the city where I was born. Being back home brought a strange comfort with it. I remember sitting at my desk one evening, the monsoon rain gently tapping the windows, and telling my parents about Steyp and the one-year tech schooling program they offered.

As always, my parents didn't just listen, they supported. I applied. I got in. And once the classes started, my life took a whole new rhythm.

Every class was like opening a door to a world I never knew existed. I started to understand design, structure, logic. But more than that, I was understanding myself. I found that I wasn't just learning to build websites, I was learning how to think like a builder, like a creator, like a problem solver.

Then, out of the blue, I got a call that I'll never forget.

It was from Steyp. They were organizing a hackathon in Alappuzha in association with Talrop's mission, Grolius. That struck a chord with me, not just because it was a great opportunity, but because Alappuzha is my father's hometown. I had family there, cousins I hadn't seen in a while. My father smiled and said, "Go for it."

CHAPTER FOUR

THE HACKATHON

I still remember that day like it was yesterday. I reached the venue early, before most others. The hall was quiet, a few chairs scattered, and I picked a spot and sat there, waiting for things to start. Slowly, the silence faded, and people started pouring in. I looked around, unfamiliar faces, confident eyes, people who looked like they already knew what they were doing.

And then, the event began.

The first person to speak was Adhil Muhammad. The moment I heard him talk, I was surprised, he was still in Higher Secondary school, but already leading a powerful mission called Grolius. That immediately grabbed my attention. A student, doing this much? I was hooked to every word he said. His energy, clarity, and ambition, it gave me a little confidence boost right at the start.

Then came the challenge.

We were asked to build a blood donation awareness website, a full 24-hour hackathon. I was teamed up with five others. At first, we were all strangers. But as soon as we started brainstorming, something clicked. Ideas started flowing. I ended up doing my first-ever pitch deck, a big moment for me. We presented our concept to the invigilators, and then dove into building the actual website.

The tension I had at the beginning slowly melted away.

We were laughing, coding, sharing snacks, discussing ideas, and even talking about our own journeys. It wasn't just a hackathon anymore. It felt like a mini-life experience, a place where I met passionate people, made new connections, and learned things textbooks could never teach.

Later that night, I got a chance to speak with the founders of Grolius. They shared their stories, their hustle, and that lit a spark in me. We had a campfire, music playing in the background, fun games, and deep conversations under the stars. It didn't feel like a competition at all, it felt like a celebration of ideas.

Even though we didn't win, something more valuable happened to me.

While I was researching for content to add on the website, I found myself copy-pasting a few lines from a site about blood donation and that's when it hit me. *There's no reliable, real-time solution for blood needs in emergencies.*

And that was it, the seed for PureLink was planted, right there, at 2 AM in the middle of a hackathon.

This experience taught me that it's not always about winning. Sometimes, it's about showing up, learning, connecting, and discovering ideas that could change lives, even your own.

I went home with a new mindset. I wanted to build a startup. I kept thinking about that blood donation platform. A few days later, I gathered the courage and called Adhil Muhammed, CEO of Grolius. I told him I had no idea how startups worked but I wanted to build one.

He simply said, "Start working on it. We'll be here to support you."

And he kept that promise.

CHAPTER FIVE

BIRTH OF PURELINK

And from there, the journey of PureLink began

I didn't know where to begin, but I knew I had to begin.

I started writing down everything. How it should work, who would use it, what features it should have. I didn't even think of it as a "startup" yet. To me, it was just solving a real problem that people face every day.

Soon, I shared the idea with a few of my friends. We were all students, all figuring things out in life but every one of us believed in the mission. Together, we built a small team. A team of dreamers. We didn't have fancy skills or big degrees. But we had purpose, and that was enough.

We didn't have much. No office, no experience, no budget. Just our laptops, a WhatsApp group, and a vision.

We'd call each other late at night and share ideas like excited kids. Some of us were learning how to code while building the app itself. Others were figuring out how to make the interface easy for someone's grandfather to use. We debated designs, user flows, color schemes, everything.

There were moments of doubt. Moments where we hit bugs we couldn't fix or days where nothing seemed to work. But there was also something bigger keeping us going, the belief that someone's life might be made a little easier because of what we were building.

And that belief? It's powerful.

Eventually, we launched our first version. It was far from perfect, but it was ours. It worked. It connected donors and receivers. It had the potential to save lives. We're now working on the second version of PureLink, with better features, a cleaner design, and a smoother user experience. We've taken every bit of feedback, every challenge we faced, and poured it into making the platform even more powerful.

Version 2 is coming soon.

Because saving lives should be simple and we're here to make that happen.

The only thing that keeps as moving is feeling of seeing our first user sign up. Or reading a message from someone saying, "Thank you, this helped." That one line, "this helped" make's every struggle worth it.

That's when it hit me: we're not just building an app. We're building hope.

PureLink is not just about technology. It's about humanity. It's about reminding ourselves that sometimes, all someone needs is a helping hand and it can come from someone just like you.

I didn't set out to build a movement. I just wanted to fix something that felt broken. But maybe that's how all great things begin with a small act, a pure intent, and a heart that refuses to stay silent.

I learned to lead. To listen. To adapt.

""Knock on every door with purpose; the right one will open when your persistence echoes loud enough.""

Doors That Didn't Open

After building the first version of PureLink, we were super excited. For us, it wasn't just some school project, we believed it could actually save lives. We knew that to make it truly useful, we had to connect it with the people who needed it the most: hospitals.

So, with nervous hearts and hopeful minds, we started reaching out to hospitals.

And reality hit us.

Most hospitals didn't even respond. Some smiled politely but didn't take us seriously, maybe because we were just teenagers, or maybe because we didn't look like the "usual tech guys." A few even said, "It's a good idea, but this won't work in the real world." It was frustrating. We had worked so hard. We had a real solution. But we couldn't find a way in.

At one point, I remember sitting outside a hospital after a meeting that didn't go well. I was tired. But something inside me whispered, "Don't stop. Even if the door doesn't open now, knock again later. Or build your own door."

That day taught me that building a solution is only part of the story, convincing others to believe in it is an entirely different journey. We started learning how to talk to professionals, how to explain things better, how to pitch with clarity. It wasn't just about coding anymore; it was about communicating.

We didn't give up.

We kept knocking.

We talked to doctors, nurses, blood bank staff, anyone who'd listen. And slowly, things started to change. Some people did listen. Some encouraged us. A few even asked us to show them how it works.

"Some doors don't open because they're waiting to see how badly you're willing to knock."

Those little wins? They felt like gold.

Even now, we're still approaching more hospitals, still improving how we present our work, and still facing challenges. But that's okay. Because that's how real change begins — not with an open door, but with the courage to knock again and again.

CHAPTER SEVEN

The Turning Point

Every startup has that one moment, a turning point where everything starts to make more sense. For us, that moment came when we met Safeer Najumudeen Sir, the CEO of Talrop.

We were a bit nervous. We had built a prototype, and we were proud of what we made. But we were also just students, unsure if our idea would really stand out. When we presented PureLink to Safeer Sir, he didn't just nod and say, "Good job." He gave us something even better, real feedback.

He showed us the flaws in our plan, and at first, it stung. But then, he broke it down for us and helped us understand how we could fix it, scale it, and make it sustainable. That day, we didn't just walk away with a better product, we walked away with a better mindset.

We were soon accepted into Talrop's incubation program. And that's when everything began to change.

At Talrop, we weren't treated like kids with a small idea. We were treated like real founders with real potential. We attended sessions, had one-on-one mentorship, and were introduced to concepts we had never heard before, startup structure, user validation, MVPs, investor readiness, business models, and product-market fit.

I remember thinking, "This is a different world. And I love it."

I learned how a startup works from the inside, how to build a team, structure a company, manage tasks, take feedback, and still stay true to your mission. We weren't just coding anymore. We were building a startup with heart, purpose, and direction.

Talrop didn't just guide us. They shaped us. From that point on, PureLink wasn't just a project, it became a mission.

""You don't build a startup just with code. You build it with courage, clarity, and community.""

CHAPTER EIGHT

FOREVER A LEARNER

When I stepped into the world of startups, I was like a traveler without a map. I didn't know what "equity" meant, had never heard of the term "MVP," and wouldn't have recognized a pitch deck if you handed one to me. Business terms sounded like a foreign language, and I had no clue how a company really worked. But instead of being scared, I was curious.

So I started learning.

YouTube became my classroom. Books became my guides. And people around me, my mentors, speakers, even fellow teens became my greatest teachers. The more I watched, listened, and read, the more I began to notice the world differently. Patterns in businesses, problems in society, solutions that could be built, all of it began to stand out like signs along a highway.

> *"Every small step forward is a step closer to success—progress, no matter how modest, is still movement toward your goal."*

I wasn't naturally a great speaker either. In fact, public speaking used to make me nervous. But I knew I had to communicate well to share my ideas. So I did what I always do: I learned. I watched great public speakers online. I observed how they moved, how they paused, how they told stories. I copied. I practiced. I failed. Then I tried again.

I still wouldn't call myself a great speaker, but I've come a long way. And that, to me, is more important than perfection.

Now, I follow a rule I've made for myself: I must learn something new every day. It doesn't have to be a big topic. Even a tiny concept or a simple idea is enough. What matters is that I stay in motion, because motion means growth.

Being a learner isn't just part of what I do. It's part of who I am now. And I know that no matter where I go or what I build, this mindset will carry me forward.

CHAPTER NINE

THE FIRST STEPS TOWARD FINANCIAL INDEPENDENCE

When I started working on my projects, I had to travel a lot to meet people, attend events, work with my team, and gather new experiences. Alongside this, I took multiple courses to sharpen my skills. All of this needed money. My parents supported me wholeheartedly. They never said no when I asked, always giving with a smile, happy to see me grow.

But over time, something started to bother me.

I realized that while they were investing in me, they were also handling the everyday responsibilities of raising three children, me and my two siblings. They were already taking care of my food, education, and other basic needs. Adding my project expenses and course fees on top of that felt unfair.

That realization changed something in me.

I decided that if I was serious about chasing my dreams, I needed to take some ownership, not just of my time and effort, but also of my expenses. That's when I turned to freelancing. I started designing posters and developing websites for clients. It wasn't easy at first, but I pushed through. Slowly, I began getting clients who trusted my work. The money I earned wasn't a fortune, but it was enough to cover my project costs and learning expenses.

I'm not fully financially independent yet, my parents still take care of my basic needs. But I've taken a step forward. I've started to reduce their burden, and that gives me a quiet sense of pride. Now, when I pay for my own courses or cover my travel expenses, it feels different. It feels earned.

More importantly, it feels like I'm becoming the person I want to be, someone who values both opportunity and responsibility.

To all the young dreamers out there: Start with something small. Try a side hustle. Whether it's designing, writing, coding, tutoring, or anything you enjoy, making even a small amount on your own builds confidence and self-respect. It's not just about money; it's about building character, learning real-world skills, and understanding the value of effort. Start now. Your future self will thank you for it.

BEYOND ONE IDEA

As PureLink moved toward launch, I realized something: this wasn't a one-time thing. I had more ideas. And I wanted to do more.

I'm now working on more startups. Each one focused on using technology to solve problems that affect people's lives. Each one guided by the same mission: to make the world a better place.

""Actually, our generation has got the power of IT. If used wisely, it can bring many positive reforms to the world.""

I believe that with the right guidance and teamwork, any dream can take form. I may still be young and learning, but this journey has given me a perspective that I wouldn't trade for anything.

CHAPTER ELEVEN

DID I MISS MY CHILDHOOD?

"Bro, you're missing out on life."

"You're always serious. You should enjoy your childhood, not work like an adult."

These are things I hear often. From friends, relatives, even strangers who learn about what I'm doing at this age. At first, I used to smile and brush it off. But somewhere deep inside, a small voice would whisper, Are they right?

While kids my age were climbing trees, going on school trips, or spending evenings playing cricket, I was on Steyp diving deep in to the world of web development. While most teens eagerly waited for the weekend to chill, I looked forward to weekends so I could plan new ideas, fix bugs, or conduct classes.

It's true, I've missed a lot of what people call "typical childhood joys." I didn't spend hours playing video games. I didn't hang out at every party. I didn't waste time scrolling endlessly on social media. I rarely even watched movies. My "free time" was usually spent learning something. And honestly, yes, sometimes it does hit me.

I see a group of friends laughing without a care in the world. I hear stories of wild, spontaneous moments and simple childhood memories that I was never part of. I've had moments where I asked myself, Did I trade something precious for something uncertain? Did I grow up too fast?

But here's the thing, I didn't exactly "lose" my childhood. I just lived it differently.

I wasn't stuck in a dull, joyless routine. In fact, I was filled with excitement. The first time I cracked a code, it felt like winning a cricket match. When I taught my first session on web development and saw students actually get it, I felt more joy than I could ever get from playing video games. When I sat up late trying to fix a database error or outline my startup structure, that was my version of "play." Because for me, exploring the world of tech and startups is fun. I didn't reject childhood. I just redefined it.

I still laughed. I still failed. I still explored. My adventures didn't happen in parks or playgrounds, they happened in the vast world of the internet, in command lines, in late-night brainstorming calls, and in turning dreams into something real.

Sometimes we think joy has only one form; playgrounds, games, parties. But joy is also curiosity. Joy is also discovery. Joy is creating something from scratch. Joy is watching your effort turn into impact.

Of course, there were sacrifices. I've had days where I felt left out. Moments where I wished I could just be a "normal kid." But those feelings never lasted long. Because every time I saw someone benefit from something I created, or when I built something I never thought I could, I realized that this path is mine.

And when people say I missed out on childhood, I smile now. Because they don't see the full picture. They see what I didn't do. But they don't see what I did.

I learned to think independently. I built skills. I met inspiring people. I failed, succeeded, and failed again—all before turning 17.

So no, I didn't lose my childhood.

> *"I didn't miss my childhood. I just spent it building the future I once dreamed of."*

I just decided to grow while others played. I chose purpose over patterns. And I found my joy in places others never thought to look.

Maybe I wasn't chasing my childhood memories, I was creating the memories that would shape my future.

CHAPTER TWELVE

A Note to My Fellow Teens

If you're between 14 and 16, here's a small piece of advice from someone walking the same road:

> *"The age you are going through is the age to get better and bigger exposure. So please don't waste this time. Use it wisely."*

You don't have to be the best in your class. You don't need to be the smartest person in the room. What you need is curiosity, courage, and consistency. The rest will follow.

Every person has a story. Mine just happens to begin with a gift, a question, and a little screen.

CHAPTER THIRTEEN

GRATITUDE

This journey wouldn't have been possible without the love, support, and belief of many people.

Thank you to:

- My Parents – for their unconditional support.
- My Co-founders at PureLink – for standing by the mission and giving it your all.
- Sobir Sir, CEO of Steyp – for being the one to build the bridge into tech.
- Safeer Sir, CEO of Talrop – for refining our vision and giving us a bigger stage.
- Adhil Muhammad and the Founders of Grolius – for introducing me to this world and never letting go of my hand.
- Yasir Muhammed – For guiding me like an elder brother.
- And all my mentors, friends, and well-wishers who believed in me when all I had was belief.

Let's continue building. Let's keep dreaming.

CHAPTER FOURTEEN

NOTE

"Stay curious, stay humble, and stay in love with the process."

-Mohamed Azvan Sait

Epilogue

This book is not the end of a journey, it's a checkpoint. I'm still learning, still building, still dreaming. My story is one of many, and if there's one thing I hope you take away, it's this:

> *"Greatness doesn't come before the first step; it follows it. Just begin, and let progress shape you."*
> — *Mohamed Azvan Sait*

We all have different beginnings, different strengths, and different paths. But what connects us is the willingness to try, to grow, and to never settle. I didn't know what a startup was when I began, but curiosity and courage brought me here. Wherever you are, your journey starts now.

Thank you for walking with me this far. I hope you find your spark, and light the way for others.

About The Author

Mohamed Azvan Sait is a passionate young changemaker, ethical hacker, and the founder of PureLink, a platform revolutionizing emergency blood donation in India. Born in India and raised in Saudi Arabia, Azvan began his journey with no technical background, only a curiosity for how things work.

By the age of 16, he had founded multiple ventures, mentored peers in cybersecurity, and turned his struggles into stepping stones. Azvan believes in learning something new every day, solving real-world problems, and being a responsible contributor to his family and society.

He hopes to inspire more students and young minds to pursue their dreams, no matter how impossible they may seem at first.

www.ingramcontent.com/pod-product-compliance
Lightning Source LLC
Chambersburg PA
CBHW021145130726
47988CB00003B/1475